SONIC:
SONIC THE HEDGEHOG HERO

★ x1991

Kenny Abdo

Fly!
An Imprint of Abdo Zoom
abdobooks.com

abdobooks.com

Published by Abdo Zoom, a division of ABDO, P.O. Box 398166, Minneapolis, Minnesota 55439. Copyright © 2021 by Abdo Consulting Group, Inc. International copyrights reserved in all countries. No part of this book may be reproduced in any form without written permission from the publisher. Fly!™ is a trademark and logo of Abdo Zoom.

Printed in the United States of America, North Mankato, Minnesota.
052020
092020

Photo Credits: Everett Collection, fandom, Flickr, Getty Images, Pond5, Shutterstock, ©DanikV p.cover / CC-BY-SA, ©BagoGames p.4, 5, 12, 16 / CC BY 2.0, ©Flickr p.5 / CC BY-ND 2.0, ©Yves Tennevin p.11 / CC BY-SA 3.0, ©Ben Wong. p.15 / CC BY-SA 3.0, ©Marco Verch p.17 / CC BY 2.0
Production Contributors: Kenny Abdo, Jennie Forsberg, Grace Hansen
Design Contributors: Dorothy Toth, Neil Klinepier

Library of Congress Control Number: 2019956166

Publisher's Cataloging-in-Publication Data

Names: Abdo, Kenny, author.
Title: Sonic: Sonic the Hedgehog hero / by Kenny Abdo
Other title: Sonic the Hedgehog hero
Description: Minneapolis, Minnesota : Abdo Zoom, 2021 | Series: Video game heroes |
    Includes online resources and index.
Identifiers: ISBN 9781098221485 (lib. bdg.) | ISBN 9781644944226 (pbk.) |
    ISBN 9781098222468 (ebook) | ISBN 9781098222956 (Read-to-Me ebook)
Subjects: LCSH: Video game characters--Juvenile literature. | Sonic the Hedgehog
    (Fictitious character)--Juvenile literature. | Hedgehogs--Juvenile literature. |
    Sega Genesis video games--Juvenile literature. | Heroes--Juvenile literature.
Classification: DDC 794.8--dc23

TABLE OF CONTENTS

SONIC THE HEDGEHOG

Collecting coins and conquering crazed doctors, Sonic the Hedgehog races past everyone else at supersonic speeds to defeat enemies!

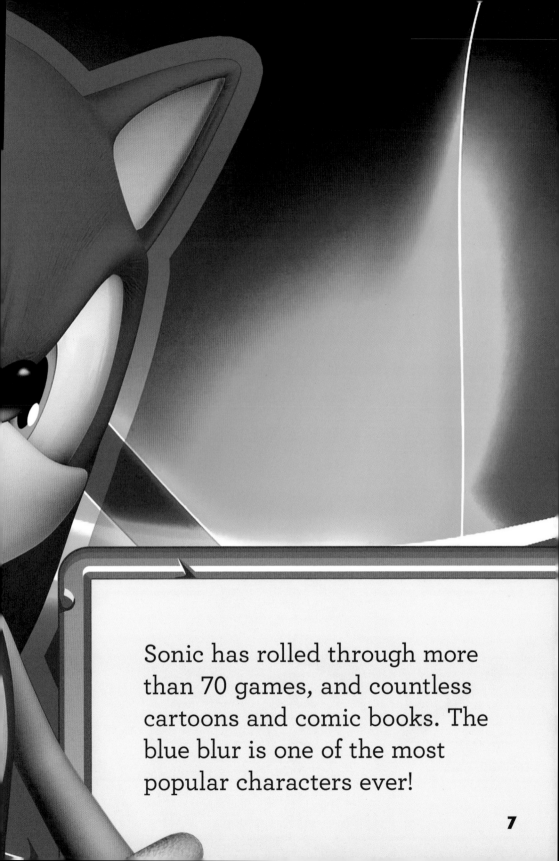

Sonic has rolled through more than 70 games, and countless cartoons and comic books. The blue blur is one of the most popular characters ever!

PLAYER PROFILE

In the early 1990s, Sega looked for a series that could outdo Nintendo's *Super Mario* game series. Japanese artist and video game designer Naoto Ohshima presented his idea. It was a speedy blue hedgehog named Mr. Needlemouse.

Mr. Needlemouse became Sonic
the Hedgehog. The character was
renamed because he could run faster
than the speed of sound.

Programmer Yuji Naka said Sonic's blue fur represented "peace, trust, and being cool." It also matched the color of Sega's logo.

LEVEL UP

Sonic the Hedgehog blew off of the shelves in 1991. The game was so popular, it helped the Sega **console** outsell the Super Nintendo. This feat was thought to be impossible.

A **sequel** was released in 1992. *Sonic the Hedgehog 2* introduced Sonic's new partner and best friend. Miles "Tails" Prower quickly became a fan favorite.

Sonic the Hedgehog 3 came out in 1994. After that, many **spin-offs** were made. Some starred Sonic. Others featured **side-characters** with brief appearances by Sonic.

Sonic the Hedgehog was **rebooted** in
2006 with better graphics and controls.
Players got to meet new characters like
Shadow and Silver.

Sonic finally went up against his rival Mario in 2007. They battled for the gold in *Mario & Sonic at the Olympic Winter Games.* The two have "competed" in each **Olympics** since.

EXPANSION PACK

In 1995, Sonic became the first
video game character to get a Macy's
Thanksgiving Day Parade balloon.

Sonic has appeared in more than 300 comic book issues. He's also starred in five cartoon series, including *Sonic X* and *Sonic Underground*.

In 2020, Sonic starred in the **live action** *Sonic the Hedgehog* movie with Jim Carrey. This video game hero can keep pace with even the biggest of Hollywood stars!

GLOSSARY

console – a type of device that you play video games on.

live action – when something drawn or animated is recreated with real people and environments.

Olympic games – the biggest sporting event in the world that is divided into summer and winter games.

reboot – a new start to a video game franchise, recreating plots, characters, and backstory.

sequel – a new game that continues the story of a previous one.

side-characters – characters that are not the main characters in a storyline.

spin-off – a certain story or game that comes from a larger story.

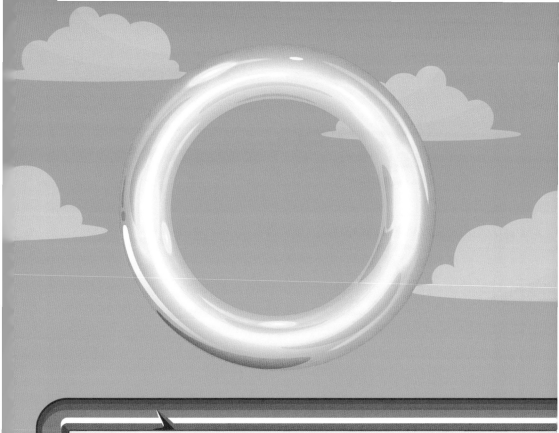

ONLINE RESOURCES

Booklinks
NONFICTION NETWORK
FREE! ONLINE NONFICTION RESOURCES

To learn more about Sonic the Hedgehog, please visit **abdobooklinks.com** or scan this QR code. These links are routinely monitored and updated to provide the most current information available.

INDEX